DATE DUE			

GYMNASTICS

Bob Bellew

The Bookwright Press
New York · 1992

Flying Start

Titles in this series

Fishing	Judo	Soccer
Gymnastics	Running	Swimming

Words in **bold** are explained in the glossary on page 30.

Cover: Elena Shoushounova, a gymnast from the Soviet Union who won an Olympic gold medal.

First published in the
United States in 1992 by
The Bookwright Press
387 Park Avenue South
New York, NY 10016

First published in 1991 by
Wayland (Publishers) Ltd
61 Western Rd, Hove
East Sussex BN3 1JD, England

Library of Congress Cataloging-in-Publication Data
Bellew, Bob.
    Gymnastics/Bob Bellew.
      p. cm.—(Flying start)
    Includes bibliographical references and index.
    Summary: Explains, to beginners, the training, equipment, and
safety precautions necessary in performing gymnastics.
    ISBN 0-531-18463-3
    1. Gymnastics—Juvenile literature. [1. Gymnastics.] I. Title.
II. Series.
GV461.B415   1992
796.44—dc20
                                                        91-9128
                                                        CIP
                                                        AC
Typesetter: Dorchester Typesetting Group Ltd.
Printer: Casterman S.A., Belgium.

CONTENTS

INTRODUCTION

You probably already swim and play tennis, soccer and baseball with your friends or at school. Perhaps you do gymnastics too. If not, have you ever thought of taking it up? Gymnastics is a lot of fun and helps you keep fit and healthy. It will teach you how to control your body, whether you are walking on your hands, jumping over a bench or playing with your friends.

When you do gymnastics your body works very hard, exercising all its different muscles and using up a lot of energy. You get much stronger and fitter.

Perhaps you already take part in gymnastics activity without really knowing it. If you look around at

Above If you enjoy doing this you will find that gymnastics is really fun.

recess you may see your friends doing handstands against a wall, playing leapfrog, doing cartwheels on the grass and skipping.

Adventure playgrounds are full of things that you can climb on, jump off and swing around from. Lots of park playgrounds have similar equipment – you can crawl, hang, swing and balance on it. All these things are linked to gymnastics. If you enjoy them, you would enjoy gymnastics as well.

Above Balancing on your hands can be tricky as well as fun.

Below Perhaps this is a future world champion!

WHERE TO GO?

Where should you go to find out more about gymnastics? You could find out if there is an after-school club by asking one of your teachers. If not, perhaps there is a club near you that you can join.

At a good gymnastics class you will be asked to do only the things you can cope with quite easily. Once you have managed these, your coach will let you try more difficult **moves**. He or she will also teach you the skills you need to be able to do difficult **routines**. These are made up of a lot of small moves that you have to learn first. Then you can fit them together into an exciting routine.

Sometimes gymnastics can be very hard, but in the end it is a lot of fun.

Bela Karolyi, a famous coach, with a young gymnast.

Gymnasts training on different pieces of apparatus.

The best thing for girls and women to wear for gymnastics is a leotard.

It is very important to wear the right clothes for gymnastics. You get very hot doing all the different activities, so you have to change into different clothes. The best clothes are comfortable ones. Make sure they are not too baggy or you might get them caught in the **apparatus** and hurt yourself.

Normally girls change into a **leotard**, which is something like a bathing suit. Boys usually wear a T-shirt and shorts. If the gym or hall is cold, you might need to wear a sweatsuit over your outfit until you get warm and then take it off.

Athletic shoes or running shoes are too heavy and clumsy for gymnastics. Bare feet are fine for most surfaces. Special gym shoes give traction and help to keep you from slipping. Be sure the slippers fit snugly and are not torn.

Boys and men usually wear shorts and a T-shirt for gymnastics.

SAFETY

● Always remember to take off jewelry, such as rings and necklaces. Jewelry could get caught on apparatus, which would be dangerous.

● If you cannot manage to get a ring off, put a piece of tape over it to protect it.

● If you have long hair, tie it back. This is to keep your hair from getting into your eyes when you are performing.

● If you need to wear glasses, make sure they are secure and cannot fall off. You can get a strap to hold them on your head.

● Your coach will check that all the apparatus is safe and secure, before you start.

Below Wrap tape around rings that cannot be removed so they do not get caught in the apparatus.

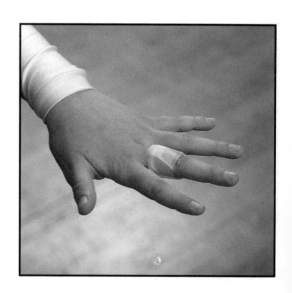

Above Wearing glasses does not stop anyone from doing gymnastics.

APPARATUS

The apparatus that you use might be a horse, low beam, single bar or small hand apparatus. Here are examples of some of the things that you might use first.

Horse

Jumping or **vaulting** over a horse or vault is fun. To begin with you might have to jump onto the vault top and then jump off again, before you try to go all the way over at once. You can make different shapes in the air when jumping off the vault.

Right This gymnast is competing in the Olympic Games in Seoul, in 1988. This type of vault is possible only after a lot of hard work.

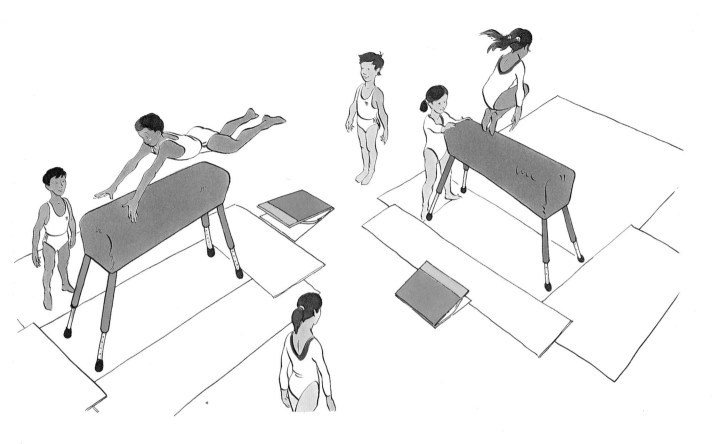

To help you get on or over the horse or vault you might use a special piece of apparatus called a **Reuther board**. This is very springy, so if you run fast before jumping onto the Reuther board you will fly through the air!

The long horse (on the left) and the broad horse (on the right).

Low beam

Walking, jumping and running along a low beam are the first things you do on this piece of apparatus. Learning to balance on a narrow piece of wood is not very easy. You will wobble a lot, or even fall off, at first. Never give up, because as you get better and gain confidence you will learn different moves. Remember to always bend your legs to cushion your landing.

Even the best gymnasts often fall off the beam. Do not give up when you are practicing on the low beam – you will get it right in the end.

Single bar

Swinging backward and forward is something every gymnast has to be good at. You can hang from a bar and make different shapes with your body. As you get better you will be able to do a circle around the bar. As a beginner you might find this the hardest piece of apparatus to use because you need lots of strength to be able to go on it.

Above   When you are learning to use the single bar you start off on a low bar.

Left   This girl is practicing swinging on the bar.

Rhythmic gymnastics

You may use pieces of small equipment in rhythmic gymnastics. These could be hoops, jumpropes or balls. They are used for swinging, circling, throwing and catching. You might also do jumprope routines.

Above Rhythmic gymnastics uses this kind of equipment.

The spotter

When you are learning a new move, or skill, a coach will usually stand close to you. This is called "spotting." It is important that the coach assists, or "spots," whenever you are learning a new skill. The **spotter** may physically help you to perform the parts of a new move. He or she also stands close enough to steady you if you slip, or to catch you if you start to fall.

Gymnasts sometimes work in teams and help one another perform exercises.

17

YOUR GYMNASTICS LESSON

Do not forget to take the right clothes. Make sure you put your bag in a safe place, ready to get changed after your lesson.

When you start the gymnastics class it is very important to warm up all of your body. If your muscles are loose you are less likely to injure yourself.

The warm-up will start with some running or jogging so that your body gets hot and you begin to pant. The running activities might be chasing or games of tag, which are fun and involve everyone. You probably already play them at school.

You must always warm up properly: even the best gymnasts get injured if they do not warm up.

After the running games, you need to warm up particular parts of your body, such as your shoulders, hips, wrists and ankles. You use these parts of your body more than others in gymnastics.

This class is warming up with their coach.

Once your whole body is warm and stretched, it is ready to use the different pieces of apparatus. You will work with other children in a group and take turns on each piece of apparatus. Normally there is a coach on each one to tell you what to do.

Once you have been on the different pieces of apparatus your coach will give you some more exercises to make your body stronger and more **flexible**. These are very important if you want your gymnastics to improve. Although some of the work may be hard, never give up, always give it a try. The stronger your body gets, the easier the skills are to perform. At the end of the lesson you will finish with some easy exercises to cool your body down.

After all that activity, it is important

Above   This girl has a very flexible back.

to change back into your normal clothes, before you go home. You will feel hot, but make sure you keep warm on your way home from the gym. Then you will not catch a cold.

Below You need to be very strong and flexible to go on the rings.

GYMNASTICS SKILLS

Which of these shapes can you make? Try to think of any other shapes that your body can make.

Forward roll

Make sure you roll on your shoulders. Keep your chin on your chest and stay in a ball shape. Reaching forward after you have rolled over will help you stand up.

Headstand

Make sure that your head is quite a long way in front of your hands. Walk in slowly toward your head until you can lift your feet off the ground. Stay in a **tuck** shape by keeping your knees on your chest. Once you can make that shape, see if you can straighten your legs and stretch out your body. Always come down in a tuck, the same way you went up, or you could hurt yourself by landing flat on your back.

Cartwheel

Try to imagine yourself cartwheeling along a straight line. Place each hand along the line and try to land your feet on it too.

Vaulting

Always bend your legs a little to cushion your landing, and then stand up. Otherwise you could hurt yourself.

You will only get really good at vaulting if you run fast and land properly, with slightly bent legs.

Below A young gymnast is helped over a horse by her coach, who makes sure she does not hurt herself.

24

Low beam

Always start on the floor, before going onto a low beam. Once you can do the move on the floor, try it on a low beam.

Never try any of these activities unless there is suitable matting and a qualified gymnastics coach present.

These German girls are very good on the beam.

A DAY AT A COMPETITION

You have probably seen gymnastics competitions on television and seen the gymnasts perform their exciting routines on all the different pieces of apparatus.

Top gymnasts come from all around the world. The Soviet Union, Romania, China and Germany are specially good at training young people to become top-class gymnasts. It takes many years of hard work to become one of the best gymnasts. Hard work could lead to your being chosen to represent your country at the **Olympic Games**. Other people enjoy just doing gymnastics with their friends and do not want to be in competitions.

In many competitions the gymnasts

Above The medal presentation at the world's biggest competition – the Olympic Games. Some day you might be able to win an Olympic medal.

perform two routines. One routine is called a **compulsory exercise** and the other an **optional exercise.** The marks from each are added together. The gymnast with the most marks is the overall winner.

Even though you will not be in front of television cameras or thousands of spectators during your first competition, it will still be an important day. Remember, all the top gymnasts started like you, in small competitions.

Above Try to remember that competitions are all meant to be fun.

Left Your first competition will probably not be in front of a camera, but you may still be nervous!

During your first competition you might feel very nervous and afraid of forgetting what you have learned. Here are some things you should try to remember.

● Show everyone that you are enjoying yourself. Gymnastics is meant to be fun.

● Listen to your coach's advice about what to do.

● Present yourself to the judges before you start your routine. This will show them that you are ready.

● Concentrate on what you are doing, not on where your family is sitting or what your friends are up to.

Above   The joy of winning.

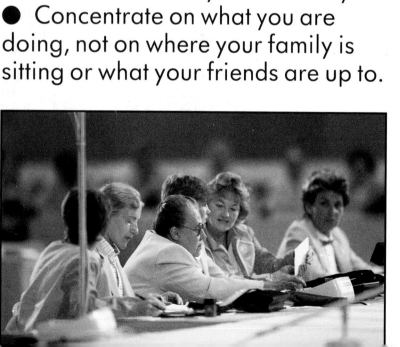

Left   The people you have to impress to win a competition – the judges.

● If you make any mistakes, do not worry, simply try to remember why you made them so that you do not do it again.

● Thank all the people who have helped you.

Lots of people never enter a competition. They prefer to see if they can win badges or certificates. A list of places you can write for more information about gymnastics is in the back of this book.

Now you know a lot more about gymnastics. You could find out where your nearest gymnastics club is and join. Or ask a teacher at your school if it would be possible to start a club after school. All your friends could join as well. You will all have a good time, and maybe one of you might end up a champion.

GOOD LUCK

One day this could be you – an Olympic champion like Ecaterino, of Romania.

Glossary

Adventure playground
A large place where there are things for children to play on. They are bigger than the playgrounds in parks and have more things to do.

Apparatus   A large object that you use to do something. The word is normally used to describe gymnastics equipment such as a vaulting horse.

Compulsory exercise   A floor routine in which all the gymnasts use the same routine.

Flexible   Easily bent. If your muscles are flexible it means you can bend your arms, legs and body without hurting yourself.

Leotard   A piece of clothing that girls and women wear for gymnastics. It looks very much like a one-piece bathing suit.

Moves   Although gymnastics often looks like one flowing movement, it is actually made up of little movements, called moves, joined together.

Olympic Games   Every four years there is a championship at which sportspeople from all around the world compete. The competition is called the Olympic Games.

Optional exercise   A floor routine in which the gymnast can make any moves he or she likes.

Reuther board   A springy board that gymnasts use when they are vaulting.

Routine   The group of moves that make up an exercise is called a routine.

Spotter   A coach who stands close to the performer. The

spotter assists the performer and helps to guard againt a fall.
Tuck The shape you make when you pull your knees into your chest.
Vaulting Jumping over a vaulting horse. There are many different ways of doing this.

Books to read

Berke, Art, *Gymnastics* (Franklin Watts, 1988)
Krementz, Jill, *A Very Young Gymnast* (Knopf, 1978)
McLaughlin, Maria, *Gymnastics* (David & Charles, 1984)
Murdock, Tony and Stuart, Nik, *Gymnastics* (1985)
Silverstein, Herma, *Mary Lou Retton and the New Gymnasts* (Franklin Watts, 1985)
Sullivan, George, *Better Gymnastics for Girls* (Putnam, 1984)
Traetta, John and Traetta, Mary Jean, *Gymnastics Basics* (Prentice Hall, 1983)

The next step

You can write to these addresses for more information about gymnastics.

U.S. Gymnastics Federation
Pan American Plaza
Suite 300
201 S. Capitol Avenue
Indianapolis
Indiana 46225

Canadian Gymnastic Federation
Suite 510
1600 James Naismith Avenue
Gloucester
Ontario K1B 5N4
Canada

Index

Numbers in **bold** indicate pictures or artwork as well as text.

Acknowledgments

All artwork was provided by Peter Parr.

The publishers would like to thank All-Sport for permission to reproduce all photographs in this book, except 4 (Eye Ubiquitous), 5 and 7 (Zefa).